The Two Ways

The Early Christian Vision of Discipleship from *The Didache* and *The Shepherd of Hermas*

Translations by Michael W. Holmes
Edited by Veery Huleatt

Introduction by Rowan Williams

PLOUGH PUBLISHING HOUSE

Published by Plough Publishing House
Walden, New York
Robertsbridge, England
Elsmore, Australia
www.plough.com

Plough produces books, a quarterly magazine, and Plough.com to encourage people and help them put their faith into action. We believe Jesus can transform the world and that his teachings and example apply to all aspects of life. At the same time, we seek common ground with all people regardless of their creed.

Plough is the publishing house of the Bruderhof, an international Christian community. The Bruderhof is a fellowship of families and singles practicing radical discipleship in the spirit of the first church in Jerusalem (Acts 2 and 4). Members devote their entire lives to serving God, one another, and their neighbors. They renounce private property and share everything. To learn more about the Bruderhof's faith, history, and daily life, see Bruderhof.com. (Views expressed by Plough authors are their own and do not necessarily reflect the position of the Bruderhof.)

Front cover photograph by Dmitry Shakin. Used by permission.
The Didache and excerpts from *The Shepherd of Hermas* are reprinted from Michael W. Holmes, editor and translator, *The Apostolic Fathers,* third edition, Baker Academic, a division of Baker Publishing Group, 2007. Used by permission.

A catalog record for this book is available from the British Library.
Library of Congress Cataloging in Publication Control Number: 2018017289 (print)

CONTENTS

THE TWO WAYS

PREFACE

How did the early Christians receive and understand the teachings of Jesus and the apostles? The writings of these believers reveal a vibrant way of discipleship concerned with all aspects of daily life: family, vocation, morality, justice, religious practice, citizenship, and leadership.

Yet despite their immediacy, these writings have for the most part remained buried in scholarly tomes, analyzed by academics but seldom used for building up the church community. Now, at a time when Christians of every persuasion are seeking clarity by returning to the roots of their faith, these simple, direct teachings can shed light on what it means to be a follower of Christ in any time or place.

This little book includes two of the earliest Christian writings outside of the New Testament: the complete text of *The Didache,* also known as *The Teaching of the Twelve Apostles,* and excerpts from *The Shepherd of Hermas,* in which the "angel of repentance" appears to Hermas, a Christian living in Rome, in the form of a shepherd. Both works were included in early lists of canonical books. They have been included here for their witness to the singular and demanding way of Jesus, reinforcing and amplifying his Sermon on the Mount with their insistence on a repentance that affects every corner of our lives.

The Didache, an anonymous work composed in the late first century AD, was lost for centuries. In 1873 Philotheos Bryennios, the metropolitan of Nicomedia, rediscovered it in an eleventh-century Greek codex at Constantinople.

The Shepherd of Hermas was written in the second century AD or possibly even earlier. The selections included here loosely follow those made by Eberhard Arnold in his 1926 omnibus of early Christian texts, which is available in English as *The Early Christians: In Their Own Words.* For Arnold, these texts were formative; they spurred him and others to start living in community after the example of these first Christians. Arnold writes: "For my own life, a clearly defined way of life and faith arises from the early Christian witness. In spite of rigidity in later centuries and changes which affected Christianity then, this way continues to be a living force today. It comes from the wellspring of living truth."

In the following introduction, Rowan Williams, former Archbishop of Canterbury, echoes Arnold, showing how unconventional and uncompromising the Christian way was in Roman times, and what it will take for Christians to reclaim this witness today: "There is all the more need for communities of believers trying to live out the radical imperatives. . . . We can't do any of this as isolated individuals with an interior piety. We need the concrete reality of Christ's corporate Body."

The English translations of the Greek are by Michael W. Holmes, a preeminent scholar of early Christianity, based on the earlier work of J. B. Lightfoot and J. R. Harmer. Those wishing to study these writings more closely – along with other significant documents of this period, notably those of Clement of Rome and Ignatius – should read Holmes's *The Apostolic Fathers,* third edition.

Veery Huleatt
Editor

INTRODUCTION

Rowan Williams

Most of the writings that survive from the first three centuries of Christianity are what one twentieth-century scholar of religion called "death-cell philosophy"; that is, they represent the kind of thinking that is done under extreme pressure, when what you say or think has a genuine life-or-death importance. Gregory Dix, an Anglican monk writing eighty or so years ago about the worship of the early church, imagined what it would be like to attend the Lord's Supper in second-century Rome by recreating the experience in terms of twentieth-century London. He takes the descriptions of worship from texts like the so-called "Teaching of the Twelve Apostles," *The Didache,* probably the most ancient account of worship outside the New Testament, and the *Apostolic Tradition* from the third century, and translates them into the landscape of modern

England. A grocer from the unfashionable suburbs slips
through the back door of a wealthy brother's house in
Kensington at the crack of dawn to share in the breaking of
bread in the drawing room – a brief, quiet event, overshad-
owed by the knowledge that if they would be discovered
they would face at least penal servitude for life, and very
likely worse. Any Christian in this period knew that, even
if things were relatively peaceful, it was always possible that
a suspicious government would crack down. Dix describes
how the "deacons," the ministers who looked after the
doors, were charged with scrutinizing everyone who came
in very carefully; you'd need to know who your companions
were if your life depended on them.

The suspicions were well-founded in one sense. If you
look at the eyewitness accounts of martyrdom in these
early centuries – documents like the wonderful record of
the martyrs of Scilli in North Africa in AD 180 – you can
see what the real issue was. These Christians, most of them
probably domestic slaves, had to explain to the magistrate
that they were quite happy to pray for the imperial state,
and even to pay taxes, but that they could not grant
the state their absolute allegiance. They had another
loyalty – which did not mean that they wished to overthrow
the administration, but that they would not comply with
the state's demands in certain respects. They would not
worship the emperor, and, as we know from some other

texts, refused to serve in the Roman army. They asked from the state what had been very reluctantly conceded to the Jews as an ethnic group – exemption from the religious requirements of the empire. What made their demand new and shocking was that it was not made on the basis of ethnic identity, but on the bare fact of conviction and conscience. For the first time in human history, individuals claimed the liberty to define the limits of their political loyalty, and to test that loyalty by spiritual and ethical standards.

That is why the early Christian movement was so threatening – and so simply baffling – to the Roman authorities. It was not revolutionary in the sense that it was trying to change the government. Its challenge was more serious: it was the claim to hold any and every government to account, to test its integrity, and to give and withhold compliance accordingly. But it would be wrong to think of this, as we are tempted to do in our era, in terms of individual conscience. It was about the right of a community to set its own standards and to form its members in the light of what had been given to them by an authority higher than the empire. The early Christians believed that if Jesus of Nazareth was "Lord," no one else could be lord over him, and therefore no one could overrule his authority. We use the word "Lord" these days mostly in a rather unthinking religious context, as a sort of devotional flourish; for a

Roman, it meant the person who made the decisions you had to abide by, from the master of a slave in the household to the emperor himself. To speak of Jesus as "King of Kings and Lord of Lords" was to say that his decisions could not be overridden by anyone. You might have to disobey a "lord" in our society in order to obey the one true Master of all – the one who used no violence in enforcing his decisions but was all the more unanswerable an authority because of that. He alone needed no reinforcement, no temporal power, to overcome external threats or rivals.

Early Christianity was on the one hand a deeply political community, posing a very specific challenge to the state by saying that the state was a provisional reality – deserving of respect and routine compliance in the ordinary affairs of social life, but having no ultimate claim. On the other hand, it was a movement fascinated by the intellectual implications of what this meant. Because if Jesus is "Lord," and if God needs no force to defend his authority against rivals, then Jesus' "policy" is God's, and Jesus shares without qualification the wisdom and self-sufficiency of God. As early as the beginning of the second century we find the martyred bishop Ignatius from Antioch calling Jesus "God"; Jesus needed no defense against rivals, and so was free to take on himself the burden of human suffering without being crushed or destroyed by it. And because of his own freedom in the face of appalling suffering, he could make it possible for his disciples to face their own suffering with the same resolution and steadiness. What Ignatius called "the passion of my God" was a gift to believers confronting those terrible risks that Gregory Dix brought alive so vividly in his study of early worshiping life.

The theology of the early centuries thus comes very directly out of this one great central conviction about political authority: if Jesus is Lord, no one else ultimately is, and so those who belong with Jesus, who share his life through the common life of the worshiping community, have a solidarity and a loyalty that goes beyond the chance identity of national or political life. The first claim on their loyalty is to live out the life of Jesus, which is also the life of God – a life that needs no defense and so has no place for violence and coercion. God, says Clement of Alexandria in the late second century, shows his love supremely in the fact that he loves people who have no "natural" claim on him. Humans love largely because of fellow-feeling, but God's love is such that it never depends on having something in common. The creator has in one sense nothing in common with his creation – how could he? But he is completely free to exercise his essential being, which is love, wherever he wills. And this teaches us that we too must learn to love beyond the boundaries of common interest and natural sympathy and, like God, love those who don't seem to have anything in common with us.

This is one of the paradoxes of early Christian thought. It's really deeply rooted in intense, mutual, disciplined community life, but at the same time insists on universal compassion and universal sympathy. The theology of the early church was not an eccentric diversion from the real business of mutual love and generous service. The doctrines of God's eternity and unchangeable consistency, the doctrine of Jesus' full participation in the divine life, ultimately the doctrine that Christians came to call the divine Trinity, and much more, derive directly from saying that Jesus is truly the supreme authority and that he exhibits exactly the same liberty to love indiscriminately as does God himself. Jesus is the earthly face of an eternal love between Father, Son, and Spirit. And when the early theologians write, as they often do, about how Christians are given a share in the divine life or the divine nature – language that can sound a bit shocking to modern believers – what they mean is simply that being in the body of Christ, in the community of baptized believers, gives us the freedom to love God the Father as Jesus loves him, through the gift of the Holy Spirit, and so too to love the world with the unquestioning generosity of God, never restricting ourselves to loving those who are familiar to us and are like us.

Writers on the life of prayer in this period – above all, the great Origen of Alexandria, who taught and wrote in

the first half of the third century – associated Christian
identity with freedom, the freedom to call God "Father"
and Jesus "Lord," as Origen puts it; which is also, for him,
a freedom from what he calls (confusingly to our ears)
"passion." This doesn't mean that Christians should have
no emotions; but that they should be free from reactive,
unthinking feelings that dictate their response to people
and things. Our response to the world around us must be
rooted in a renewal of our minds, seeing through superficial
differences to recognize God's presence and purpose in all
persons and things.

And for all these great figures, there were blindingly
obvious practical implications – to treat each other with
forgiveness and respect, to address poverty and suffering,
and to step back from the institutions of the state, espe-
cially the army. None of this was fully encoded in rules, but
the church expected people to be able to draw the obvious
conclusions from the simple starting point of living under a
new authority. We know that there were Christian soldiers
in those centuries, but we know too that the community in
general never settled happily with the idea that Christians
should bear arms. Origen is one of the many who could
not be reconciled to that idea. And even when things were
beginning to change drastically in the fourth century,
with a Christian emperor who sounded increasingly like
his non-Christian predecessors, there were figures like
Martin of Tours in France who discovered, when they

converted, that they couldn't carry on as soldiers. Even the formidable Augustine of Hippo at the beginning of the fifth century – famous as the man who first outlined the conditions for a "just war" – is crystal clear that, while he thinks Christians may take part in defensive war to protect the weak, we should never try to defend the gospel by war. It's a pity that this side of Augustine's thought was largely overlooked by people eager to make him an ally of just those imperial military myths that he was so regularly scathing about.

We have to admit that, by the fifth century, the church *was* looking different. Having become legal at the beginning of the fourth century, it steadily became more and more involved with the power of the state and was seen as giving legitimacy to the emperor. Those who argued for this were neither wicked nor hypnotized by power and influence (though no doubt some had their temptations). They thought that divine providence had at last put an end to their cruel sufferings and provided them with an ally in the Christian emperor. Augustine is one of those who disagreed strongly with this, but not many took up his approach. For most, it was easier to believe that God had brought human history nearer its fulfillment by converting the power of the state. And it was when all this was going on that some serious Christians started moving away from cities and towns to become monks in the deserts of Egypt and Syria – so that they could reconstruct the life of the first believers in Jerusalem, sharing their property and living in simplicity. For many centuries, indeed, the life of the monks was described as the "apostolic" life. And originally it was a life for laypeople, not clergy; those who became monks were as eager to escape from the hierarchy of the church as from the hierarchy of the state. In the sermons and stories that were developed in this setting, we find the same themes that appear in earlier writing: the common life of Christians must display the characteristics of the life of the Lord, in unquestioning compassion and mercy, in generosity and simplicity, and in refusing to defend oneself or compare oneself with others.

In this period, the great central theme of Christian existence was how to live in such a way that it was clear where one's loyalty lay – because this was the best way of witnessing to a God whose eternal life was utterly free from competition and conflict. The experience of a new way of living in community prompted theological questioning; the theological clarifications reinforced and deepened the sense of the priorities and imperatives for the community. One of the lasting legacies of the early church, then, is the recognition that doctrine, prayer, and ethics don't exist in tidy separate compartments: each one shapes the others. And in the church in any age, we should not be surprised if we become hazy about our doctrine at a time when we are less clear about our priorities as a community, or if we become less passionate about service, forgiveness, and peace when we have stopped thinking clearly about the true and eternal character of God.

We don't have to be uncritical of the Christians in that early period. But what they offer us is a clear message about how Christian identity is always a claim to a "citizenship" that is deeper and more universal than any human society can provide. Christians are always going to be living at an angle to the mainstream – not claiming a glib moral superiority, yet insisting that they "march to a different drum" since they recognize final and unsurpassable authority in the living and dying of Jesus of Nazareth. He, they insisted, is the only one who has the right and the liberty to tell us what is real and true in the universe. This does not mean that the church is locked in a violent contest with state or society, that it is struggling for supremacy. If Christ is who we believe him to be, there is never any need for struggle; nothing will make him less real or true. Insofar as there is a struggle, it is against our own willingness to let other authorities overrule Christ. In the early church, that was a life-and-death matter – and it still is for Christians in some parts of the world today.

For most of us the consequences are less dramatic, but the challenge is still there. Our faith is still a "death-cell philosophy," certainly in a world that confuses "life" with victory, prosperity, or security at the expense of others. We know better what life really is – what must be let go of in order for it to flourish, what astonishing gifts are opened up for those who find the courage to step beyond what is conventionally and religiously taken for granted. And if the struggle is hard – as it is, even if we are not threatened with martyrdom – there is all the more need for communities of believers trying to live out the radical imperatives: communities of monastic discipline in the old way, new communities focused on peace and the disciplines of nonviolence. We can't do any of this as isolated individuals with an interior piety. We need the concrete reality of Christ's corporate Body, nourished by his Supper.

The thinking of the Christians of those first few centuries – their letters, their sermons, their forms of worship, and even sometimes their fierce arguments about doctrine – shows us how theology and discipleship are closely interwoven. For them, theology was not a luxury or an academic affair, it was their way of discerning more clearly what their way of life demanded. That integrated sense of mind, will, and heart exploring together is something we can still learn from these great figures who often at the greatest personal risk discovered with joy what Christ asked of them and discovered with surprise what they were capable of in response. Reason enough for reading them again with eagerness and enthusiasm.

THE DIDACHE

*The Teaching of the Lord
to the Gentiles by the Twelve Apostles*

The Two Ways

There are two ways, one of life and one of death, and there is a great difference between these two ways.

The First Commandment of the Way of Life

Now this is the way of life: First, you shall love God, who made you. Second, you shall love your neighbor as yourself; but whatever you do not wish to happen to you, do not do to another. The teaching of these words is this: Bless those who curse you, and pray for your enemies, and fast for those who persecute you. For what credit is it if you love those who love you? Do not even the Gentiles do the same? But you must love those who hate you, and you will not have an enemy. Abstain from fleshly and bodily cravings. If someone gives you a blow on your right cheek, turn to him the other as well and you will be perfect. If someone forces you to go one mile, go with him two miles; if someone takes your cloak, give him your tunic also; if someone takes from you what belongs to you, do not demand it back, for you cannot do so. Give to everyone who asks you, and do not demand it back, for the Father wants something from his own gifts to be given to everyone. Blessed is the one who gives according to the command, for such a person is innocent. Woe to the one who receives: if, on the one hand, someone who is in need receives, this person is innocent, but the one who does not have need will have to explain why and for what purpose he received, and upon being imprisoned will be interrogated about what he has done, and will not be released from there until he has repaid every last cent. But it has also been said concerning this: "Let your gift sweat in your hands until you know to whom to give it."

The Second Commandment of the Way of Life

The second commandment of the teaching is: You shall not murder; you shall not commit adultery; you shall not corrupt children; you shall not be sexually immoral; you shall not steal; you shall not practice magic; you shall not engage in sorcery; you shall not abort a child or commit infanticide. You shall not covet your neighbor's possessions; you shall not commit perjury; you shall not give false testimony; you shall not speak evil; you shall not hold a grudge. You shall not be double-minded or double-tongued, for the double tongue is a deadly snare. Your word must not be false or meaningless, but confirmed by action. You shall not be greedy or avaricious, or a hypocrite or malicious

4

or arrogant. You shall not hatch evil plots against your neighbor. You shall not hate any one; instead you shall reprove some, and pray for some, and some you shall love more than your own life.

To Do and Not Do

My child, flee from evil of every kind and from everything resembling it. Do not become angry, for anger leads to murder. Do not be jealous or quarrelsome or hot-tempered, for all these things breed murders. My child, do not be lustful, for lust leads to sexual immorality. Do not be foul-mouthed or let your eyes roam, for all these things breed adultery. My child, do not be an augur, since it leads to idolatry. Do not be an enchanter or an astrologer or a magician, or even desire to see them, for all these things breed idolatry. My child, do not be a liar, since lying leads to theft. Do not be avaricious or conceited, for all these things breed thefts. My child, do not be a grumbler, since it leads to blasphemy. Do not be arrogant or evil-minded, for all these things breed blasphemies.

Instead, be humble, for the humble shall inherit the earth. Be patient and merciful and innocent and quiet and good, and revere always the words that you have heard. Do not exalt yourself or permit your soul to become arrogant. Your soul shall not associate with the lofty, but live with the righteous and the humble. Accept as good the things that happen to you, knowing that nothing transpires apart from God.

My child, remember night and day the one who preaches God's word to you, and honor him as though he were the Lord. For wherever the Lord's nature is preached, there the Lord is. Moreover, you shall seek out daily the presence of the saints, so that you may find support in their words. You shall not cause division, but shall make peace between those who quarrel. You shall judge righteously; you shall not show partiality when reproving transgressions. You shall not waver with regard to your decisions.

Do not be one who stretches out the hands to receive but withdraws them when it comes to giving. If you earn something by working with your hands, you shall give a ransom for your sins. You shall not hesitate to give, nor shall you grumble when giving, for you will know who is the good paymaster of the reward. You shall not turn away from someone in need, but shall share everything with your brother or sister, and do not claim that anything is your own. For if you are sharers in what is imperishable, how much more so in perishable things!

You shall not withhold your hand from your son or your daughter, but from their youth you shall teach them the fear of God. You shall not give orders to your male slave or female servant (who hope in the same God as you) when you are angry, lest they cease to fear the God who is over you both. For he comes to call not with regard to reputation but those whom the Spirit has prepared. And you slaves shall be submissive to your masters in respect and fear, as to a symbol of God.

You shall hate all hypocrisy and everything that is not pleasing to the Lord. You must not forsake the Lord's commandments but must guard what you have received, neither adding nor subtracting anything. In church you shall confess your transgressions, and you shall not approach your prayer with an evil conscience. This is the way of life.

The Way of Death

But the way of death is this: first of all, it is evil and completely cursed; murders, adulteries, lusts, sexual immoralities, thefts, idolatries, magic arts, sorceries, robberies, false testimonies, hypocrisies, duplicity, deceit, pride, malice, stubbornness, greed, abusive language, jealousy, audacity, arrogance, boastfulness. It is the way of persecutors of good people, of those who hate truth, love a lie, do not know the reward of righteousness, do not adhere to what is good or to righteous judgment, who are vigilant not for what is good but for what is evil, from whom gentleness and patience are far removed, who love worthless things, pursue a reward, have no mercy for the poor, do not work on behalf of the oppressed, do not know the one who made them, are murderers of children, corrupters of God's creation, who turn away from someone in need, who oppress the afflicted, are advocates of the wealthy, lawless judges of the poor, utterly sinful. May you be delivered, children, from all these things!

The Right Choice

See that no one leads you astray from this way of the teaching, for such a person teaches you without regard for God. For if you are able to bear the whole yoke of the Lord, you will be perfect. But if you are not able, then do what you can.

Concerning Food

Now concerning food, bear what you are able, but in any case keep strictly away from meat sacrificed to idols, for it involves the worship of dead gods.

Concerning Baptism

Now concerning baptism, baptize as follows: after you have reviewed all these things, baptize in the name of the Father and of the Son and of the Holy Spirit in running water. But if you have no running water, then baptize in some other water; and if you are not able to baptize in cold water, then do so in warm. But if you have neither, then pour water on the head three times in the name of Father and Son and Holy Spirit. And before the baptism let the one baptizing and the one who is to be baptized fast, as well as any others who are able. Also, you must instruct the one who is to be baptized to fast for one or two days beforehand.

Concerning Fasts

But do not let your fasts coincide with those of the hypocrites. They fast on Monday and Thursday, so you must fast on Wednesday and Friday.

Concerning Prayer

Nor should you pray like the hypocrites. Instead, pray like this, just as the Lord commanded in his Gospel:

Our Father in heaven,
hallowed be your name,
your kingdom come,
your will be done on earth as it is in heaven.
Give us today our daily bread,
and forgive us our debt, as we also forgive our debtors;
and do not lead us into temptation,

but deliver us from the evil one;
for yours is the power and the glory forever.

Pray like this three times a day.

Concerning the Eucharist

Now concerning the Eucharist, give thanks as follows.
First, concerning the cup:

We give you thanks, our Father,
for the holy vine of David your servant,
which you have made known to us
through Jesus, your servant;
to you be the glory forever.

And concerning the broken bread:

We give you thanks, our Father,
for the life and knowledge
that you have made known to us
through Jesus, your servant;
to you be the glory forever.

Just as this broken bread was scattered upon the mountains and then was gathered together and became one,
so may your church be gathered together from the ends of
the earth into your kingdom;

for yours is the glory and the power through Jesus Christ
forever.

But let no one eat or drink of your Eucharist except those
who have been baptized into the name of the Lord, for the
Lord has also spoken concerning this: "Do not give what is
holy to dogs."

And after you have had enough, give thanks as follows:

We give you thanks, Holy Father,
for your holy name, which you have caused to dwell in our
hearts,
and for the knowledge and faith and immortality that you
have made known to us through Jesus your servant;
to you be the glory forever.
You, almighty Master, created all things for your name's
sake,
and gave food and drink to humans to enjoy, so that they
might give you thanks;
but to us you have graciously given spiritual food and
drink,
and eternal life through your servant.
Above all we give thanks to you because you are mighty; to
you be the glory forever.
Remember your church, Lord,
to deliver it from all evil and to make it perfect in your
love;

and from the four winds gather the church that has been
    sanctified into your kingdom,
which you have prepared for it;
for yours is the power and the glory forever.
May grace come, and may this world pass away.
Hosanna to the God of David.
If anyone is holy, let him come;
if anyone is not, let him repent.
Maranatha! Amen.

But permit the prophets to give thanks however they wish.

Concerning Teachers

So, if anyone should come and teach you all these things
that have just been mentioned above, welcome him. But
if the teacher himself goes astray and teaches a different
teaching that undermines all this, do not listen to him.
However, if his teaching contributes to righteousness and
knowledge of the Lord, welcome him as you would the Lord.

Concerning Itinerant Apostles and Prophets

Now concerning the apostles and prophets, deal with them
as follows in accordance with the rule of the gospel. Let
every apostle who comes to you be welcomed as if he were
the Lord. But he is not to stay for more than one day, unless

there is need, in which case he may stay another. But if he stays three days, he is a false prophet. And when the apostle leaves, he is to take nothing except bread until he finds his next night's lodging. But if he asks for money, he is a false prophet. Also, do not test or evaluate any prophet who speaks in the spirit, for every sin will be forgiven, but this sin will not be forgiven. However, not everyone who speaks in the spirit is a prophet, but only if he exhibits the Lord's ways. By his conduct, therefore, will the false prophet and the prophet be recognized. Furthermore, any prophet who orders a meal in the spirit shall not partake of it; if he does, he is a false prophet. If any prophet teaches the truth, yet does not practice what he teaches, he is a false prophet. But any prophet proven to be genuine who does something with a view to portraying in a worldly manner the symbolic meaning of the church (provided that he does not teach you to do all that he himself does) is not to be judged by you, for his judgment is with God. Besides, the ancient prophets also acted in a similar manner. But if anyone should say in the spirit, "Give me money" or anything else, do not listen to him. But if he tells you to give on behalf of others who are in need, let no one judge him.

Everyone who comes in the name of the Lord is to be welcomed. But then examine him, and you will find out – for you will have insight – what is true and what is false. If the one who comes is merely passing through, assist him as much as you can. But he must not stay with you for more than two or, if necessary, three days. However, if he wishes to settle among you and is a craftsman, let him work for his living. But if he is not a craftsman, decide according to your own judgment how he shall live among you as a Christian, yet without being idle. But if he does not wish to cooperate in this way, then he is trading on Christ. Beware of such people.

But every genuine prophet who wishes to settle among you is worthy of his food. Likewise, every genuine teacher is, like the worker, worthy of his food. Take, therefore, all the first fruits of the produce of the wine press and threshing floor, and of the cattle and sheep, and give these first fruits to the prophets, for they are your high priests. But if you have no prophet, give them to the poor. If you make bread, take the first fruit and give in accordance with the commandment. Similarly, when you open a jar of wine or oil, take the first fruit and give it to the prophets. As for money and clothes and any other possessions, take the first fruit that seems right to you and give in accordance with the commandment.

Concerning the Lord's Day

On the Lord's own day gather together and break bread and give thanks, having first confessed your sins so that your sacrifice may be pure. But let no one who has a quarrel with a companion join you until they have been reconciled, so that your sacrifice may not be defiled. For this is the sacrifice concerning which the Lord said, "In every place and time offer me a pure sacrifice, for I am a great king, says the Lord, and my name is marvelous among the nations."

Bishops and Deacons

Therefore appoint for yourselves bishops and deacons worthy of the Lord, men who are humble and not avaricious and true and approved, for they too carry out for you the ministry of the prophets and teachers. You must not, therefore, despise them, for they are your honored men, along with the prophets and teachers.

Call to Follow the Gospel

Furthermore, correct one another not in anger but in peace, as you find in the Gospel; and if anyone wrongs his or her neighbor, let no one speak to that person, nor let that one hear a word from you, until he or she repents. As for your prayers and acts of charity and all your actions, do them all just as you find it in the Gospel of our Lord.

Watch over your life: do not let your lamps go out, and do not be unprepared, but be ready, for you do not know the hour when our Lord is coming. Gather together frequently, seeking the things that benefit your souls, for all the time you have believed will be of no use to you if you are not found perfect in the last time.

The Last Days

For in the last days the false prophets and corrupters will abound, and the sheep will be turned into wolves, and love will be turned into hate. For as lawlessness increases, they will hate and persecute and betray one another. And then the deceiver of the world will appear as a son of God and will perform signs and wonders, and the earth will be delivered into his hands, and he will commit abominations the likes of which have never happened before. Then all humankind will come to the fiery test, and many will fall away and perish; but those who endure in their faith will be saved by the accursed one himself. And then there will appear the signs of the truth: first the sign of an opening in heaven, then the sign of the sound of a trumpet, and third, the resurrection of the dead – but not of all; rather, as it has been said, "The Lord will come, and all his saints with him." Then the world will see the Lord coming upon the clouds of heaven.

THE SHEPHERD
OF HERMAS

The Shepherd of Hermas *narrates several revelations or visions (and the explanations of their meaning and significance) given to Hermas, a Christian living in Rome; the visions typically are mediated and explained by an angelic figure. The document takes its name from a key figure in the book, the "angel of repentance," who appears to Hermas in the form of a shepherd. The selections that follow are from chapters 10–17, 25–30, 33–50, 53–55, 79–84, 86, 109, and 114.*

The Tower and the Stones

In one vision, Hermas sees an elderly woman. He is told that the woman is the church, and that she appears thus because "she was created before all things; therefore she is elderly, and for her sake the world was formed." The elderly woman speaks to Hermas.

She said to me, "Look! Do you not see right in front of you a great tower being built upon the waters out of shining square stones?" And the tower was being built in a square by the six young men who had come with her, and countless other men were bringing stones, some of them from the deep and some from the land, and they were giving them to the six young men. And they were taking them and were building. All the stones that were dragged from the deep they placed in the building just as they were, for they had been shaped and fit at the joints with the other stones. In fact, they fitted one another so closely that the joints were not visible, and the structure of the tower looked as if it were built of a single stone. But of the other stones that were brought in from the dry land, some they threw away, and some they placed in the building, and others they broke in pieces and threw far away from the tower. And many other stones were lying around the tower, and they were not using them for the building, for some of them were damaged and others had cracks in them, and others were too short and others were white and round, and did not fit into the building. And I saw other stones thrown far from the tower and coming onto the road yet not staying on the road, but rolling to the wasteland; and others were falling into the fire and burning, and others were falling near the water, yet were not able to roll into the water, even though they wanted to roll and to come to the water.

When she had shown me these things she wished to hurry away. I said to her, "Lady, what good does it do me to have seen these things and yet not know what they mean?" Answering me, she said, "You are a crafty fellow, wanting to know all about the tower."

"Yes, lady," I replied, "so that I may report to my brothers and sisters, and so that they may be cheered, and that as a result of hearing these things they may know the Lord in much glory."

Then she said, "Many will hear; but after hearing, some of them will rejoice, but others will weep. Yet even these, if they hear and repent, will also rejoice. Hear, therefore, the parables of the tower, for I will reveal everything to you.

And do not bother me any more about a revelation, for these revelations have come to an end, for they have been completed. But you will never stop asking for revelations, for you are shameless. The tower that you see being built is I, the church, who appeared to you now and previously. So ask whatever you want about the tower, and I will reveal it to you, so that you may rejoice with the saints."

I said to her, "Lady, since you once considered me worthy to reveal everything to me, reveal it."

And she said to me, "Whatever can be revealed to you will be revealed. Only let your heart be with God, and do not be double-minded about what you see."

I asked her, "Why is the tower built upon water, lady?"

"As I said to you before," she said, "you do seek diligently. By seeking, therefore, you are finding the truth. Hear, then, why the tower is built upon water: it is because your life was saved and will be saved through water. But the tower has been set on a foundation by the word of the almighty and glorious Name, and is strengthened by the unseen power of the Master."

I answered and said to her, "Lady, this thing is great and marvelous. But who are the six young men who are building, lady?"

"These are the holy angels of God who were created first of all, to whom the Lord committed all his creation to increase and to build up, and to rule over all creation. Through them, therefore, the construction of the tower will be completed."

"And who are the others who are bringing the stones?"

"They too are holy angels of God, but these six are superior to them. The construction of the tower will be completed, and all will rejoice together around the tower and will glorify God because the construction of the tower was completed."

I inquired of her, saying: "Lady, I wish to know about the destination of the stones, and what kind of meaning they have."

Answering me she said, "It is not because you are worthier than all others to have it revealed to you, for others are before you and are better than you, to whom these visions ought to have been revealed. But it has been revealed to you in order that the name of God might be glorified, and it will be revealed for the sake of the double-minded, who question in their hearts whether or not these things are so. Tell them that all these things are true, and that there is nothing besides the truth, but all are powerful and reliable and firmly established."

"Now hear about the stones that go into the building. The stones that are square and white and fit at their joints, these are the apostles and bishops and teachers and deacons who have walked according to the holiness of God and have

ministered to the elect of God as bishops and teachers
and deacons with purity and reverence; some have fallen
asleep, while others are still living. And they always agreed
with one another, and so they had peace with one another
and listened to one another. For this reason their joints fit
together in the building of the tower."

"But who are the ones that are dragged from the deep
and placed in the building, whose joints fit together with
the other stones already used in the building?"

"They are those who have suffered for the name of the
Lord."

"And I wish to know who are the other stones brought
from the dry land, lady."

She said, "Those going into the building without being
hewn are those whom the Lord has approved because
they walked in the uprightness of the Lord and rightly
performed his commandments."

"And who are the ones who are being brought and placed
in the building?"

"They are young in faith, and faithful; but they are
warned by the angels to do good, because wickedness was
not found in them."

"Who are the ones they rejected and threw away?"

"They are the ones who have sinned and wish to repent.
Therefore they were not thrown far from the tower, because
they will be useful for building if they repent. So, then, the
ones who are about to repent, if in fact they do repent, will

be strong in the faith if they repent now while the tower is still being built. But if the tower is finished, they will no longer have a place, but will be rejects. The only advantage they have is this, that they lie near the tower."

"And do you want to know who are the ones that are broken in pieces and thrown far away from the tower? These are the children of lawlessness; they believed hypocritically, and no wickedness escaped them. Therefore they do not have salvation, because they are not useful for building on account of their wickedness. That is why they were broken up and thrown far away, because of the Lord's wrath, for they angered him. As for the others that you saw lying around in great numbers and not going into the building, the ones that are damaged are those who have known the truth but did not abide in it, nor do they associate with the saints. Therefore they are useless."

"But who are the ones with cracks?"

"These are the ones who have something against one another in their hearts and are not at peace among themselves. Instead, they have only the appearance of peace, and when they leave one another their evil thoughts remain in their hearts. These are the cracks that the stones have. The ones that are too short are those who have believed and live for the most part in righteousness, but they have a certain amount of lawlessness; that is why they are too short and not perfect."

"And who are the white and round stones that do not fit into the building, lady?"

She answered and said to me, "How long will you be foolish and stupid, asking about everything and understanding nothing? These are the ones who have faith, but also have the riches of this world. Whenever persecution comes, they deny their Lord because of their riches and their business affairs."

And I answered her and said, "Then when, lady, will they be useful for the building?"

"When," she replied, "their riches, which lead their souls astray, are cut away, then they will be useful to God. For just as the round stone cannot become square unless it is trimmed and loses some part of itself, so also those who are rich in this world cannot become useful to the Lord unless their riches are cut away. Learn first from yourself: when you were rich, you were useless, but now you are useful and beneficial to life. Be useful to God, for you yourself are to be used as one of these stones."

"And the other stones that you saw thrown far from the tower, and falling onto the road and rolling off the road to wastelands, are those who have believed but because of their double-mindedness abandon their true road. Thinking that they can find a better way, they go astray and wander about in misery, trudging through the wastelands. Those falling into the fire and burning are those who have completely rebelled against the living God, and the thought no longer enters their heart to repent on account of their licentious desires and the evil deeds they do. And do you want to know who are the ones that fall near the waters but are not able to roll into the water? They are the ones who heard the word and want to be baptized in the name of the Lord. Then, when they remember the purity of the truth, they change their mind and return again to their evil desires." . . .

Then I began to ask her about the times, in particular if the consummation had already arrived. But she cried out in a loud voice, saying: "You foolish man, can you not see that the tower is still being built? When the tower is finished being built, then the end comes. But it will be built up quickly. Do not ask me any more questions; this reminder and the renewal of your spirits is sufficient for you and for the saints. But these things have not been revealed for you alone, but in order that you might show them to everyone. After three days – for you must first understand it yourself – I command you first, Hermas, to speak all these words that I am about to tell you to the ears of the saints, in order that by hearing and doing them they may be cleansed from their wickedness, and you with them."

"Listen, my children. I brought you up in much sincerity and innocence and reverence through the mercy of the Lord, who instilled righteousness in you in order that you may be justified and sanctified from all evil and from all perversity. Yet you do not want to cease from your wickedness. Now listen to me and be at peace among yourselves, and be concerned for one another and assist one another; and do not partake of God's creation in abundance by yourselves, but also share with those in need. For by overeating some people bring on themselves fleshly weaknesses and injure their flesh, while the flesh of those who do not have anything to eat is injured because they do not have enough food, and their bodies are wasting away. This lack of community spirit is harmful to those of you who have, yet do not share with those in need. Look to the coming judgment. You, therefore, who have more than enough, seek out those who are hungry, until the tower is finished. For after the tower is finished, you may want to do good, but you will not have the chance. Beware, therefore, you who exult in your wealth, lest those in need groan, and their groaning rise up to the Lord, and you together with your good things be shut outside the door of the tower." . . .

Commandments of the Shepherd

After I had prayed in my house and sat down on my bed, there came a man glorious in appearance, dressed like a shepherd, with a white skin wrapped around him and with a bag on his shoulders and a staff in his hand. He greeted me, and I greeted him in return. He immediately sat down beside me and said to me, "I was sent by the most holy angel to live with you the rest of the days of your life." . . . So I wrote down the commandments and parables, just as he commanded me. If, then, when you hear them you keep them and walk in them and carry them out with a clean heart, you will receive from the Lord whatever he promised you. But if after hearing them you do not repent, but continue to add to your sins, you will receive from the Lord the opposite. All these things the shepherd, the angel of repentance, commanded me to write as follows.

COMMANDMENT 1

Faith in God

"First of all, believe that God is one, who created all things and set them in order, and made out of what did not exist everything that is, and who contains all things but is himself alone uncontained. Believe in him, therefore, and fear him, and fearing him, exercise self-control. Observe these things, and you will cast off all evil from yourself and will put on every virtue of righteousness and will live to God, if you observe this commandment."

COMMANDMENT 2

Sincerity and Innocence

He said to me: "Be sincere and be innocent, and you will be like little children who do not know the evil that destroys human life. First, speak evil of no one, and do not enjoy listening to someone who does. Otherwise you, the listener, will be responsible for the sin of the one speaking evil, if you believe the slander that you have heard, for by believing it you yourself will hold a grudge against your brother or sister. In this way you will become responsible for the sin of the one who speaks the evil. Slander is evil; it is a restless demon, never at peace but always at home with dissension. So avoid it, and you will always have success with everyone. Clothe yourself with reverence, in which there is no evil cause for offense, but all things are smooth and joyful. Work at what is good, and out of your labor, which God gives you, give generously to all who are in need, not debating to whom you will give and to whom you will not. Give to all, for God wishes that from his own gifts, gifts should be given to all. So those who receive are accountable to God regarding why they received and to what end; for those in distress who receive will not be judged, but those who receive under false pretenses will pay the penalty. Therefore those who give are innocent, for as they received from the Lord a ministry to carry out, they carried it out sincerely, not worrying about to whom to give or not to give. This ministry, then, when sincerely carried out, becomes glorious in God's sight. Therefore the one who serves God sincerely in this manner will live. So keep this commandment, as I have told you, in order that your repentance and that of your family may prove to be sincere and pure and innocent and unstained."

COMMANDMENT 3

Love the Truth

Again he spoke to me: "Love truth, and allow only the truth to come from your mouth, in order that the spirit that God caused to live in this flesh may prove to be true in the sight of all people; and thus will the Lord who lives in you be glorified. For the Lord is truthful in every word, and there is nothing false in him. Therefore, those who lie reject the Lord and defraud the Lord, for they do not return to him the deposit that they received. For they received from him a spirit uncontaminated by deceit. If they return this as a lying spirit, they have polluted the Lord's commandment and become thieves."

When I heard these things, I wept bitterly. But when he saw me weeping, he said, "Why are you crying?"

"Because, sir," I said, "I do not know if I can be saved."

"Why?" he asked.

"Because, sir," I replied, "never in my life have I spoken a true word; instead, I have lived deceitfully with everyone, and have represented my lie as truth to everyone, and no one ever contradicted me but believed my word. So how," I said, "can I live after having done these things?"

"Your thinking," he said, "is right and true, for you must, as God's servant, live truthfully, and an evil conscience must not live with the spirit of truth or bring grief to the spirit that is holy and true."

"Never before, sir," I said, "have I correctly heard such words."

"Well," he said, "you are hearing them now. . . . If you obey these and from now on speak only the truth, you will be able to attain life for yourself. And whoever hears this commandment and has nothing to do with falsehood, that most pernicious habit, will live to God."

COMMANDMENT 4

Purity and Repentance

"I command you," he said, "to guard purity, and let no thought enter your heart about another man's wife or about fornication, or about some such similar evil thing, for in doing this you commit a great sin. But always keep your mind on your own wife and you will never go wrong. For if this desire enters your heart, you will go wrong, and if other things as evil as this enter, you commit sin. For this desire in a servant of God is a great sin, and if anyone does this evil deed, he brings death on himself. So beware! Have nothing to do with this desire; for where holiness lives, there lawlessness ought not to enter the heart of a righteous person. . . . As for his or her previous sin, there is One who is able to give healing; it is he who has authority over everything."

I asked him again, saying, "Since the Lord considered me worthy for you to live with me always, allow me a few more words, since I do not understand anything and my heart has been hardened by my previous deeds. Make me understand, because I am very foolish and comprehend absolutely nothing."

He answered me and spoke thus: "I," he said, "am in charge of repentance, and I give understanding to all who repent. Or do you not think," he said, "that this very act of repentance is itself understanding? To repent," he continued, "is great understanding. For those who have sinned understand that they have done evil in the Lord's presence, and the act that they committed enters their heart, and they repent and no longer do evil, but do good lavishly, and they humble their own soul and torment it, because they sinned. You see, therefore, that repentance is great understanding."

"This, sir," I said, "is why I question you so precisely about everything; first, because I am a sinner; and second, because I do not know what deeds I must do in order to live, because my sins are many and varied."

"You will live," he said, "if you obey my commandments and walk in them. And whoever hears these commandments and obeys them will live to God." . . .

COMMANDMENT 5

Patience and Anger

"Be patient and understanding," he said, "and you will overcome all evil deeds and will accomplish all righteousness. For if you are patient, the holy spirit that lives in you will be pure, uncontaminated by some other, evil spirit;

living in a spacious room, it will rejoice and be glad with
the vessel in which it lives, and will serve God with much
cheerfulness, for it is at peace with itself. But if an angry
temper approaches, immediately the holy spirit, which is
very sensitive, is distressed because it does not have a clean
place, and it seeks to leave the place. For it is choked by the
evil spirit and does not have the room to serve the Lord the
way it wants to, because it is polluted by the angry temper.
For the Lord lives in patience, but the devil lives in an angry
temper. So if both spirits live together, it is unfortunate
and evil for that person in whom they live. For if you take a
little wormwood and pour it in a jar of honey, all the honey
is spoiled, is it not? Such a large amount of honey spoiled by
such a small amount of wormwood; it spoils the sweetness,
and the owner no longer cares for it, because it has become
bitter and lost its usefulness. But if the wormwood is not
put into the honey, the honey turns out to be sweet and
is useful to its owner. You see, then, that patience is very
sweet, even more so than honey, and is useful to the Lord,
and he lives in it. But an angry temper is bitter and useless.
So, if an angry temper is mixed with patience, the patience
is polluted, and its intercession is no longer useful to God."

"I would like to know, sir," I said, "how an angry temper
works, in order that I can protect myself from it."

"Indeed," he said, "if you do not protect yourself and
your family from it, you have lost all hope. But protect
yourself from it, for I am with you. And all who repent with

all their heart will protect themselves from it, for I will be with them and will keep them safe, for they were all justified by the most holy angel."

"Now hear," he said, "how an angry temper works, how evil it is, and how it subverts God's servants by its working, and how it leads them astray from righteousness. But it does not lead astray those who are filled with faith, nor can it work on them, because the Lord's power is with them. But it can lead astray those who are empty-headed and double-minded. For whenever it sees such people prospering, it insinuates itself into the person's heart, and for no reason at all the man or the woman is embittered over worldly concerns, either about food or something trivial, or some friend, or about giving or receiving, or foolish matters such as these. For these things are all foolish and empty and senseless and inexpedient for God's servants. But patience is great and strong, and possesses a mighty and vigorous power, and prospers in a spacious area; it is joyful, exultant, free from care, glorifying the Lord at all times, having no bitterness in itself, always remaining gentle and quiet. This patience, therefore, lives with those whose faith is perfect. But an angry temper is first of all foolish, fickle, and senseless. Then from foolishness comes bitterness, and from bitterness wrath, and from wrath anger, and from anger vengefulness. Then vengefulness, being composed of all these evil elements, becomes a great and incurable sin. For when all these spirits live in one vessel, where the holy spirit also lives, the vessel cannot contain them, but overflows. So the sensitive spirit, which is used to living neither with an evil spirit nor with harshness, departs from a person such as this and seeks to live with gentleness and quiet. Then, when it has left the one in whom it lives, that person is emptied of the spirit of righteousness, and from then on, since he or she is filled with the evil spirits, that one is unstable in everything he or she does and is dragged about here and there by the evil spirits, totally blind with respect to good intentions. So it goes, therefore, with all those who are ill-tempered. Have nothing to do, therefore, with an angry temper, that most evil spirit. Instead, put on patience and resist an angry temper and bitterness, and you will be found in the company of the holiness that is loved by the Lord. So take care that you never neglect this commandment, for if you master it, you will also be able to keep the rest of the commandments that I am about to give you. Be strong in them, and empowered; indeed, let all who want to walk in them be empowered."

COMMANDMENT 6

Two Ways

"I commanded you," he said, "in the first commandments to protect faith and fear and self-control."

"Yes, sir," I said.

"But now," he said, "I want to explain to you their powers, so that you may understand what the power and effect of each of them is. For their effects are twofold; they relate to righteousness and to unrighteousness. Be sure, therefore, to trust righteousness, but do not trust unrighteousness. For the way of righteousness is straight, but the way of unrighteousness is crooked. But follow the straight and level way, and leave the crooked one alone. For the crooked way has no paths but only uneven ground and many obstacles, and is rough and thorny. Consequently, it is harmful to those who follow it. But those who follow the straight path walk smoothly and without stumbling, for it is neither rough nor thorny. You see, then, that it is more advantageous to follow this way."

"I am pleased, sir," I said, "to follow this way."

"So follow it," he said, "and whoever turns to the Lord wholeheartedly will follow it."

Two Angels

"Now hear," he said, "about faith. There are two angels with a person, one of righteousness and one of wickedness."

"So how, sir," I said, "will I recognize their workings, given that both angels live with me?"

"Listen," he said, "and you will understand them. The angel of righteousness is sensitive and modest and gentle and tranquil. When this one enters your heart, immediately he talks with you about righteousness, about purity, about holiness, about contentment, about every righteous deed, and about every glorious virtue. Whenever all these things enter your heart, you know that the angel of righteousness is with you. These, then, are the works of the angel of righteousness. So trust him and his works. Now observe the works of the angel of wickedness. First of all, he is ill-tempered and bitter and senseless, and his works are evil, tearing down God's servants. So whenever this one enters your heart, recognize him by his works."

"But I do not know, sir," I said, "how to recognize him."

"Listen," he said. "When some angry temperamental outburst or bitterness comes over you, recognize that he is in you. Then comes the desire for much business, and extravagant kinds of food and drink, and much drunkenness, and various kinds of unnecessary luxuries, and the desire for women, and greed and arrogance and pretentiousness, and whatever else resembles or is similar to these things. So whenever these things enter your heart, you know that the angel of wickedness is with you. Recognizing, therefore, his works, shun him and do not trust him at all, because his works are evil and harmful to God's servants. You now have, then, the working of both angels; understand them and trust the angel of righteousness. But shun the angel of wickedness, because his teaching is evil in every respect. For if there should be an extremely faithful man, and the thought of that angel should enter his heart, that man – or woman – must inevitably commit some sin. On the other hand, if there should be an extremely sinful man or woman, and the works of the angel of righteousness should enter his or her heart, of necessity that person must do something good. You see, then," he said, "that it is good to follow the angel of righteousness but shun the angel of wickedness. This commandment explains the things about faith, in order that you may trust the works of the angel of righteousness, and that doing them, you may live to God. But believe that the works of the angel of wickedness are dangerous, so that by not doing them you will live to God."

COMMANDMENT 7

Fear the Lord

"Fear the Lord," he said, "and keep his commandments. By keeping his commandments, you will be powerful in every deed, and your activity will be beyond criticism. For when you fear the Lord you will do everything well. This is the fear you must have to be saved. But do not fear the devil, for if you fear the Lord you will rule over the devil, because he has no power. And where there is no power, there is no fear. But where there is glorious power, there also is fear. For everyone who has power has fear, whereas the one who has no power is despised by everyone. But fear the works of the devil, because they are evil. When you fear the Lord you will fear the devil's works and will not do them, but will have nothing to do with them. Fear, therefore, is of two kinds. If you want to do something evil, fear the Lord and you will not do it. But on the other hand, if you want to do good, fear the Lord and you will do it. So, the fear of the Lord is powerful and great and glorious. Fear the Lord, therefore, and you will live to him; and whoever fears the Lord and keeps his commandments will live to God."

"Why, sir," I said, "did you say about those keeping his commandments, 'they will live to God'?"

"Because," he replied, "every creature fears the Lord, but not all keep his commandments. Life with God, therefore, belongs to those who fear him and keep his commandments; but those who do not keep his commandments do not have life in him, either."

COMMANDMENT 8

Self-Control

"I mentioned to you," he said, "that the creatures of God are twofold, because self-control is also twofold. For in some things it is necessary to exercise self-control, but in some things it is not necessary."

"Inform me, sir," I said, "about what things it is necessary to practice self-control and in what things it is not necessary."

"Listen," he said. "Be self-controlled regarding evil, and do not do it; but do not be self-controlled regarding good, but do it. For if you exercise self-control regarding what is good and do not do it, you commit a great sin. But if you exercise self-control regarding evil so as not to do it, you achieve great righteousness. Exercise self-control, therefore, over all evil and do what is good."

"Sir," I responded, "what are the kinds of evils over which it is necessary for us to exercise self-control?"

"Listen," he said: "adultery and fornication, lawless drunkenness, wicked luxury, many kinds of food and the extravagance of wealth and boasting and snobbery and arrogance, and lying and slander and hypocrisy, malice and all blasphemy. These actions are the most wicked of all in human life. So, the servant of God must exercise self-control over these works, for the one who does not exercise self-control over these is not able to live to God. Listen also, therefore, to the things that follow them."

"Why, sir," I said, "are there still other evil practices?"

"Indeed, there are many," he said, "over which the servant of God must exercise self-control: theft, lying, robbery, perjury, greed, lust, deceit, vanity, pretentiousness, and whatever else is like these. Do you not think that these things are evil? Indeed, to the servants of God they are very evil," he said. "In all these things the one who serves God must exercise self-control. Exercise self-control, therefore, over all these things, so that you may live to God and be enrolled with those who do exercise self-control over them. These, then, are the matters in which you must exercise self-control."

"But now listen," he said, "to those things in which you must not exercise self-control, but do them. Do not exercise self-control over the good, but do it."

"Explain to me," I said, "the power of the good things also, so that I may walk in them and serve them, in order that by doing them I may be able to be saved."

"Hear," he said, "about the works of the good things, which you must do and toward which you must not exercise self-control. First of all, there is faith, fear of the Lord, love, harmony, words of righteousness, truth, patience; nothing is better than these in human life. Those who keep these things and do not exercise self-control over them will be blessed in their life. Next hear the things that follow these: serving widows, looking after orphans and those in need, delivering God's servants from distress, being hospitable (for the practice of hospitality results in doing good, I presume), opposing no one, being quiet, becoming more needy than all other men, respecting the elderly, practicing righteousness, preserving the bond of fellowship, enduring insults, being patient, bearing no grudges, encouraging those who are sick at heart, not throwing out those who have stumbled but turning them around and encouraging them, admonishing sinners, not oppressing debtors and those in need, and whatever else is like these. Do you not think," he said, "that these things are good?"

"Why sir," I replied, "what can be better than these?"

"Then walk in them," he said, "and do not exercise self-control over them, and you will live to God. So keep this commandment; if you do good and do not exercise self-control in this respect, you will live to God; indeed, all who do so will live to God. And again, if you do not do evil and do exercise self-control over it, you will live to God; indeed, all who keep these commandments and walk in them will live to God."

COMMANDMENT 9

Double-Mindedness

He said to me, "Rid yourself of double-mindedness, and do not be at all double-minded about asking God for something, saying to yourself, for example, 'How can I ask for something from God and receive it, when I have sinned so often against him?' Do not reason in this way, but turn to the Lord with all your heart and ask of him unhesitatingly, and you will know his extraordinary compassion, because he will never abandon you but will fulfill your soul's request. For God is not like humans, who bear grudges; no, he is without malice and has compassion on his creation. You, therefore, cleanse your heart of all the vanities of this life, and of all the things mentioned to you above, and ask of the Lord, and you will receive everything, and will not fail to receive all of your requests, if you ask unhesitatingly. But if you hesitate in your heart, you will certainly not receive any of your requests. For those who hesitate in their relation to God are the double-minded, and they never obtain any of their requests. But those who are perfect in faith make all their requests trusting in the Lord, and they receive them, because they ask unhesitatingly, without any double-mindedness. For any double-minded person who does not repent will scarcely be saved.

"So cleanse your heart of double-mindedness and put on faith, because it is strong, and trust God that you will receive all the requests you make. And whenever you ask for something from the Lord and you receive your request rather slowly, do not become double-minded just because you did not receive your soul's request quickly, for assuredly it is because of some temptation or some transgression, of which you are ignorant, that you are receiving your request

44

rather slowly. Do not stop, therefore, making your soul's request, and you will receive it. But if you become weary and double-minded as you ask, blame yourself and not the one who gives to you. Beware of this double-mindedness, for it is evil and senseless, and has uprooted many from the faith, even those who are very faithful and strong. For this double-mindedness is indeed a daughter of the devil, and does much evil to God's servants. So despise double-mindedness and gain mastery over it in everything by clothing yourself with faith that is strong and powerful. For faith promises all things, perfects all things; but double-mindedness, not having any confidence in itself, fails in all the works it tries to do. So you see," he said, "that faith is from above, from the Lord, and has great power, but double-mindedness is an earthly spirit from the devil that has no power. So serve faith, which has power, and have nothing to do with double-mindedness, which has no power, and you will live to God; indeed, all who are so minded will live to God."

COMMANDMENT 10

Cheerfulness and Grief

"Rid yourself," he said to me, "of grief, for it is the sister of double-mindedness and an angry temper."

"Sir," I asked, "how is it the sister of these? For an angry temper seems to me to be one thing, double-mindedness another, and grief another."

"You are a foolish man," he said. "Do you not understand that grief is the most evil of all the spirits and very bad for God's servants, and that it corrupts a person more than all the spirits and crushes the holy spirit, and saves again?"

"I am foolish, sir," I said, "and I do not understand these parables. For how it can both corrupt and save again, I do not comprehend."

"Listen," he said. "Those who have never searched for the truth or inquired about the deity, but have simply believed, and have been entangled in business affairs and wealth and friendships with outsiders and many other concerns of this world – well, those who are absorbed in these things do not comprehend the divine parables, because they are darkened by these matters and are ruined and become barren. Just as good vineyards are made barren by thorns and weeds of various kinds when they are neglected, so people who have believed and then fall into these many activities that have been mentioned above lose their understanding and do not comprehend anything at all concerning righteousness. For whenever they hear about divine matters and truth, their mind is preoccupied with their own affairs, and they understand nothing at all. But those who fear God and inquire about divine matters and truth and direct their heart to the Lord grasp more quickly and understand everything that is said to them, because they have the fear of the Lord in themselves; for where the Lord lives, there also is much understanding. So hold fast to the Lord and you will understand and grasp everything."

"Foolish man," he said, "hear now how grief crushes the holy spirit and saves again. Whenever double-minded people undertake some action and fail at it because of their double-mindedness, this grief enters them and grieves the holy spirit and crushes it. Then again, when an angry temper holds fast to people over some matter and they become very embittered, again grief enters the heart of the angry-tempered ones, and they are grieved by what they have done, and they repent because they have done evil. This grief, therefore, seems to bring salvation, because they repented after having done evil. So, both actions grieve the spirit: the double-mindedness, because it did not succeed in its attempt, and the angry temper grieves the spirit, because it did what was evil. So both are a cause for grief for the holy spirit, double-mindedness and an angry temper. Rid yourself, therefore, of grief and do not oppress the holy spirit that lives in you, lest it intercede with God against you and leave you. For the spirit of God that was given to this flesh endures neither grief nor distress. Clothe yourself,

therefore, with cheerfulness, which always finds favor
with God and is acceptable to him, and rejoice in it. For all
cheerful people do good things and think good things, and
despise grief." ...

COMMANDMENT 11

Discerning True and False Prophets

He showed me people seated on a bench, and another
person seated on a chair. And he said to me, "Do you see
those people seated on the bench?"

"I see them, sir," I replied.

"These," he said, "are faithful, but the one seated on the
chair is a false prophet who destroys the mind of God's
servants; that is, he destroys the mind of the double-
minded, not of believers. The double-minded come to him
as to a fortune-teller and ask him what will happen to them.
And that false prophet, not having the power of a divine
spirit in himself, answers them in accordance with their
questions and their wicked desires, and fills their souls
just as they themselves wish. For since he himself is empty,
he gives empty answers to empty inquirers, for no matter
what is asked, he answers according to the emptiness of
the one asking. But he does speak some true words, for
the devil fills him with his own spirit, to see if he will be
able to break down any of the righteous. So, those who are

strong in the faith of the Lord, having clothed themselves with the truth, do not associate with such spirits, but have nothing to do with them. But those who are double-minded and frequently change their minds practice fortune-telling like the outsiders and bring greater sin upon themselves by their idolatries. For the one who consults a false prophet on any matter is an idolater and lacks the truth and is senseless. For no spirit given by God needs to be consulted; instead, having the divine power, it speaks everything on its own initiative, because it is from above, from the power of the divine spirit. But the spirit that is consulted and that answers according to the desires of the people consulting it is earthly and fickle, and has no power, and does not speak at all unless it is consulted."

"So how, sir," I asked, "will a person know which of them is a prophet and which is a false prophet?"

"Hear," he said, "about both the prophets, and on the basis of what I am going to tell you, you can test the prophet and false prophet. Determine the man who has the divine spirit by his life."

The True Prophet

"In the first place the one who has the divine spirit from above is gentle and quiet and humble, and stays away from all evil and futile desires of this age, and considers himself to be poorer than others, and gives no answer to anyone when consulted. Nor does he speak on his own (nor does the holy spirit speak when a person wants to speak), but when God wants him to speak. So, then, when the person who has the divine spirit comes into an assembly of righteous people who have faith in a divine spirit, and intercession is made to God by the assembly of those people, then the angel of the prophetic spirit that is assigned to him fills the person, and being filled with the holy spirit the man speaks to the multitude just as the Lord wills. In this way, then, the divine spirit will be obvious. Such, therefore, is the power of discernment with respect to the divine spirit of the Lord."

The False Prophet

"Now hear," he said, "about the earthly and worthless spirit, which has no power but is foolish. In the first place, that person who seems to have a spirit exalts himself and wants to have a seat of honor, and immediately is arrogant and shameless and talkative and well-acquainted with many luxuries and with many other pleasures, and receives money for his prophesying, and if he does not receive money, he does not prophesy. Now, can a divine spirit receive money and still prophesy? It is impossible for a prophet of God to do this, but the spirit of such prophets who do so is earthly. Next, he never comes near an assembly of righteous people; instead he avoids them, and associates with the double-minded and the empty-headed, and prophesies to them in a corner and deceives them; everything he says is

in accordance with their own desires and characterized by
his own empty manner, for he is answering those who are
empty. For the empty vessel placed together with other
empty vessels is not broken, but they match one another.
But when he does come to an assembly full of righteous
people who have a divine spirit, and intercession is made
by them, that person is emptied and the earthly spirit flees
from him in fear, and that person is rendered speechless
and is completely shattered, unable to say a thing." . . .

The Power of the Spirit

"Take a stone and throw it toward the sky; see if you can
reach it. Or, for another example, take a water pump and
squirt it toward the sky; see if you can penetrate it."

"How," I asked, "can these things be, sir? For both these
things you just said are impossible."

"Well then," he said, "just as these things are impossible,
so also are the earthly spirits powerless and weak. Now
consider the power that comes from above. A hailstone is
a very small pellet, but when it falls on a man's head, what
pain it causes! Or, for another example, take a drop that
falls on the ground from the roofing tiles, and wears a hole
in the rock. You see, then, that even the smallest things
from above falling on the earth have great power; so also
the divine spirit that comes from above is powerful. So put
your trust in this spirit, but have nothing to do with the
other one."

COMMANDMENT 12

Evil and Good Desires

He said to me, "Rid yourself of all evil desire, and clothe yourself with the desire that is good and holy, for when you have clothed yourself with this desire, you will hate the evil desire and will control it as you wish. For the evil desire is savage and only tamed with difficulty, for it is terrible and utterly destroys people by its savageness; in particular, if servants of God become entangled in it and lack understanding, they will be terribly destroyed by it. It destroys those who do not have the garment of the good desire but are entangled with this world. These it hands over to death."

"What, sir," I said, "are the works of this evil desire that hand people over to death? Tell me, so that I may avoid them."

"Hear," he said, "about the kind of works by which the evil desire puts to death God's servants."

"Above all is the desire for someone else's wife or husband, and for the extravagance of wealth, and for many needless things to eat and drink, and for many other foolish luxuries. For every luxury is foolish and empty for God's servants. These desires, then, are evil and bring death to God's servants. For this evil desire is a daughter of the devil. You must keep away, therefore, from evil desires, in order that by keeping away from them you may live to God. But those who are mastered by them and do not resist them will utterly perish, for these desires are deadly. But put on the desire of righteousness and, having armed yourself with the fear of the Lord, resist them. For the fear of God lives in the good desire. If the evil desire sees you armed with the fear of God and resisting it, it will flee far from you and will no longer be seen by you, because it fears your weapons. So you, when you have gained the victory and triumphed over the evil desire, come to the desire of righteousness and deliver to it the victory you have won, and serve it just as it desires. If you serve the good desire and submit to it, you will be able to master the evil desire and control it as you wish." . . .

On Keeping These Commandments

So he finished the twelve commandments, and said to me: "You have the commandments; walk in them and encourage your listeners, in order that their repentance may be pure the rest of the days of their lives. Carefully execute this ministry that I am giving you and you will accomplish much. For you will find favor with those who are going to repent, and they will obey your words, for I will be with you and will compel them to obey you."

I said to him, "Sir, these commandments are great and good and glorious, and are able to gladden the heart of the one who is able to keep them. But I do not know if these commandments can be kept by a human, for they are very hard."

He answered and said to me, "If you propose to yourself that they can be kept, you will keep them easily and they will not be hard. But if the idea that they cannot be kept by a human has already entered your heart, you will not keep them. But now I say to you: if you do not keep them, but neglect them, you will not have salvation, nor will your children nor your household, since you have already decided for yourself that these commandments cannot be kept by a human."

He said these things to me very angrily, which confused me, and I feared him greatly, for his appearance was so changed that one could not endure his anger. And when he saw that I was extremely agitated and confused, he began to speak to me more gently and cheerfully, and said, "Foolish man, lacking understanding and double-minded, do you not understand how great and mighty and marvelous God's glory is, because he created the world for the sake of humankind, and subjected all his creation to humankind, and gave them all authority to rule over everything under heaven? If then," he said, "humankind is lord of all God's creatures and rules over everything, cannot humankind also master these commandments? Those who have the

Lord in their heart," he said, "can master everything, including all these commandments. But to those who have the Lord on their lips but whose heart is hardened and who are far from the Lord, these commandments are hard and difficult. You, therefore, who are empty and fickle in the faith, put the Lord in your heart and you will realize that nothing is easier or sweeter or more gentle than these commandments. You who walk in the commandments of the devil, which are difficult and bitter and savage and licentious, be converted and do not fear the devil, for he has no power against you. For I, the angel of repentance, rule over him; I will be with you. The devil can only cause fear, but his fear has no force. Do not fear him, therefore, and he will flee from you." ...

"Sir," I said, "everyone is eager to keep God's commandments, and there is no one who does not ask the Lord to be strengthened in his commandments and obey them, but the devil is hard and oppresses them."

"He cannot," he said, "oppress God's servants who hope in him with all their heart. The devil can wrestle with them, but he cannot throw and pin them. So, if you resist him, he will be defeated and flee from you in disgrace. But those," he said, "who are empty fear the devil, as if he had power. When someone fills a large number of jars with good wine, and among these jars a few are partially empty, he does not bother to examine the full jars when he comes to the jars, for he knows that they are full. But he does examine the partially empty ones because he fears that they may have turned sour. For partially empty jars quickly turn sour, and the taste of the wine is ruined. So also the devil comes to all God's servants to tempt them. All those who are full in the faith resist him mightily, and he leaves them alone, because he finds no place where he can gain entrance. So then he comes to those who are partially empty, and finding a place he enters them, and then he does what he wants with them, and they become enslaved to him."

"But I, the angel of repentance, say to you: do not fear the devil. For I was sent," he said, "to be with you who repent with all your heart, and to strengthen you in the faith. So believe in God, you who because of your sins have despaired of your life and are adding to your sins and making your life hard, because if you turn to the Lord with all your heart and practice righteousness the rest of the days of your life and serve him rightly according to his will, he will heal your previous sins and you will have power to conquer the devil's works. But do not fear the devil's threats at all, for he is as powerless as a dead man's sinews. Listen to me, therefore, and fear the one who is able to do everything, to save and to destroy, and keep these commandments, and you will live to God."

Parables of the Shepherd

Two Cities

He spoke to me: "You know," he said, "that you who are servants of God are living in a foreign country, for your city is far from this city. If, therefore, you know," he said, "your city in which you are destined to live, why do you prepare fields and expensive possessions and buildings and useless rooms here? If you are preparing these things for this city, you obviously are not planning to return to your own city. Foolish and double-minded and miserable person, do you not realize that all these things are foreign to you, and under someone else's authority? For the lord of this city will say, 'I do not want you to live in my city; instead, leave this city, because you do not conform to my laws.' So, you who have fields and dwellings and many other possessions, what will you do with your field and your house and all the other things you have prepared for yourself when you are expelled by him? For the lord of this country has every right to say to you, 'Either conform to my laws, or get out of my country.' So what are you going to do, since you are subject to the law of your own city? For the sake of your fields and the rest of your possessions, will you totally renounce your own law and live according to the law of this city? Take care; it may not be in your best interest to renounce your law, for if you should want to return to your city, you will certainly not be accepted, because you have renounced the law of your city, and will be shut out of it.

"So take care; as one living in a foreign land, do not prepare for yourself one thing more than is necessary to be self-sufficient, and be prepared so that whenever the master of this city wants to expel you because of your opposition to his law, you can leave his city and come to your own city, and joyfully conform to your law, free from all insult. Take care, therefore, that you serve the Lord and have him in your heart; do God's works, remembering his commandments and the promises that he made, and trust him to keep them, if his commandments are kept. So instead of fields, buy souls that are in distress, as anyone is able, and visit widows and orphans, and do not neglect them; and spend your wealth and all your possessions, which you received from God, on fields and houses of this kind. For this is why the Master made you rich, so that you might perform these ministries for him. It is much better to purchase fields and possessions and houses of this kind, which you will find in your own city when you go home to it. This lavish expenditure is beautiful and joyous; it does not bring grief or fear, but joy. So do not practice the extravagance of the outsiders, for it is unprofitable to you, the servants of God. But do practice your own extravagance, in which you can rejoice; and do not imitate or touch what belongs to another or covet it, for it is evil to covet someone else's things. But do your own task, and you will be saved." . . .

Trees in Winter

He showed me many trees that had no leaves, and they appeared to me to be withered, for they were all alike. . . . He said, "These trees that you see are the people who live in this world."

"So why, sir," I asked, "do they look like they are withered and all alike?"

"Because," he said, "neither the righteous nor sinners are distinguishable in this world, but they are alike. For this world is winter to the righteous, and they cannot be distinguished, because they live with the sinners. For just as in winter the trees, having shed their leaves, are all alike, and it is not apparent which are withered and which are living, so also in this world neither the righteous nor the sinners can be distinguished, but all are alike."

Trees in Summer

Again he showed me many trees, some of which were budding and some of which were withered. . . . "These trees," he said, "that are budding are the righteous, who will live in the age to come; for the age to come is summer to the righteous but winter to the sinners. So when the mercy of the Lord shines forth, then those who serve God will be revealed; indeed, all people will be revealed. For just as in summer the fruit of each one of the trees appears, and so it is known what kind they are, so also the fruit of the righteous will be revealed, and all will be known because they are flourishing in that world. But the outsiders and the sinners, the withered trees that you saw, will be found to be withered and fruitless in that world, and will be burned as firewood, and will be obvious because their conduct in their life was evil. For the sinners will be burned because they sinned and did not repent, and the outsiders will be burned because they did not know the one who created them. You, therefore, bear fruit, in order that in summer your fruit may be known." . . .

The Vineyard

As I was fasting while sitting on a certain mountain and giving thanks to the Lord for all that he had done for me, I saw the shepherd sitting next to me, and he said, "Why have you come here so early?"

"Because, sir," I replied, "I have a station."

"What," he said, "is a 'station'?"

"Sir," I replied, "I am fasting."

"And what," he continued, "is this fast you are keeping?"

"I am fasting, sir," I responded, "just as I have been accustomed to."

"You do not know," he said, "how to fast to God, and this useless fast that you are keeping for him is not a fast."

"Sir," I said, "why are you saying this?"

"I am telling you," he said, "that even though you think you are fasting, this is not a fast. But I will teach you what a complete and acceptable fast to the Lord is."

"Yes, sir," I said. "You will make me happy if I may learn about the fast acceptable to God."

"Listen," he said. "God does not desire such a worthless fast as this, for by fasting to God in this manner, you are accomplishing nothing with respect to righteousness. But keep a fast to God in this way: Commit no evil in your life, and serve the Lord with a clean heart; keep his commandments and walk in his ordinances, and do not permit any evil desire to enter your heart, and believe in God. And if you do these things and fear him and restrain yourself from every evil deed, you will live to God; and if you do these things, you will complete a fast that is great and acceptable to God.

"Listen to the parable that I am about to tell you about fasting. A certain man had a field and many slaves, and in a part of the field he planted a vineyard. And as he was going away on a journey, he chose a certain slave who was trustworthy and pleasing to him and called him over and said to him, 'Take this vineyard that I have planted and fence it in until I return, but do not do anything else to the vineyard. Obey this command of mine, and you will gain your freedom from me.' Then the slave's master went away on a journey. When he had gone, the slave took and fenced in the vineyard. When he finished fencing in the vineyard, he noticed that the vineyard was full of weeds. So he thought to himself, saying, 'This command of the lord I have carried out. Next I will cultivate this vineyard; indeed, it will look better after it is cultivated, and, having no weeds, it will yield more fruit, because it will not be choked by weeds.' So he took and cultivated the vineyard, and pulled out all the weeds that were in the vineyard, and the vineyard was very attractive and flourishing, because no weeds were choking it.

"Some time later, the master of the slave and of the field returned, and he went to the vineyard. And when he saw the vineyard fenced in neatly, and cultivated as well, and all the weeds pulled out, and the vineyard flourishing, he rejoiced greatly at what his slave had done. So he called his beloved son, who was his heir, and his friends, who were his advisers, and told them what he had commanded his servant to do and what he had found done. And they congratulated the slave on the testimony that his master gave him. And he said to them, 'I promised this slave his freedom if he obeyed the command that I gave him. He has obeyed my command, and has, to my great pleasure, done a good job in the vineyard besides. Therefore, in return for this work that he has done, I wish to make him joint heir with my son, because when the good idea occurred to him, he did not ignore it but did it.' The master's son agreed with his decision that the slave should become joint heir with the son.

"A few days later his master gave a feast and sent him a considerable amount of food from the feast. But when the slave received the food sent to him by the master, he took enough for himself and distributed the rest to his fellow slaves. And when his fellow servants received the food, they rejoiced and began to pray for him, in order that he might find even greater favor with the master, because he had treated them so well. His master heard about all these things that had happened, and again he rejoiced greatly at his conduct. Calling together again his friends and son, he reported to them what the slave had done with the food that he had received, and they all the more heartily approved of the slave's being made a joint heir with his son." . . .

Building the Tower

The shepherd shows Hermas a great plain surrounded by twelve mountains and explains the meaning of each.

And in the middle of the plain he pointed out to me a great white rock rising up from the plain. And the rock was higher than the mountains and square, so that it could hold the whole world. And that rock was old, and a door had been chiseled out of it; but the door seemed to me to have been chiseled out quite recently. And the door was so much more radiant than the sun that I marveled at the brightness of the door. Around the door stood twelve virgins. The four who stood at the corners seemed to me to be more glorious (though the others were also glorious), and they stood at the four sides of the door, with a pair of virgins between each of them. And they were dressed in linen tunics that were becomingly belted around them, their right shoulders bare, as though they were about to carry some load. . . .

I saw that six men had come, tall and glorious and similar in appearance, and they called a multitude of men. And those who came were also tall men, handsome and powerful. And the six men ordered them to build a tower upon the rock. And there arose a great noise from those men who had come to build the tower as they ran here and there around the door. And the virgins standing around the door were telling the men to hurry to build the tower, and the virgins spread out their hands as though they were about to receive something from the men. And the six men ordered stones to come up from some deep place and to go into the structure of the tower. And ten square stones, polished and unhewn, came up. And the six men called the virgins and ordered them to pick up all the stones that were to go into the structure of the tower and to pass through the door and hand them to the men who were about to build the tower. And the virgins put the first ten stones that arose from the deep on one another, and they carried them together, stone by stone.

In the same order in which they stood together around the door, those who seemed to be the strongest picked up the stone and got under its corners, while the others got under the sides of the stone, and thus they carried all the stones. They carried them through the door, just as they were ordered, and handed them to the men for the tower, and they took them and built. The tower was built upon the great rock and above the door. So those ten stones were fitted together, and they covered the whole rock. And these formed the foundation for the construction of the tower; the rock and the door were supporting the whole tower. And after the ten stones, twenty-five other stones came up from the deep, and these were fitted into the structure of the

tower, having been carried in by the virgins like the previous
ones. And after these thirty-five came up, and these were
likewise fitted into the tower. After these, forty other stones
came up, and these were all put into the structure of the
tower. So four tiers were laid in the foundations of the
tower. And the stones stopped coming up from the deep,
and the builders also stopped for a little while. And next
the six men ordered the multitude of the people to bring
in stones from the mountains for the construction of the
tower. So stones of various colors were brought in from
all the mountains, having been quarried by the men, and
handed to the virgins, and the virgins carried them through
the door and handed them over for the construction of
the tower. And when the various stones were set into the
building, they all alike became white and lost their various
colors. But some of the stones that were delivered by the
men for the building did not become bright, but were found
to be the same color as when they were put in; for they were
not handed along by the virgins, nor had they been carried
through the gate. These stones, therefore, were unsuitable
for the building of the tower. When the six men saw the
unsuitable stones in the building, they ordered them to be
removed and taken down to their own place, from where
they had been brought. And they said to the men who were
bringing in the stones, "You must not bring any stones at all
into the building, but only place them by the tower, so that
the virgins can carry them through the door and hand them

over for the building. For if," they said, "they are not carried through the gate by the hands of these virgins, they cannot change their colors. So do not labor in vain," they said.

And the construction was finished for that day, though the tower was not yet completed, for it was to be built up further, and there was a pause in the construction. And the six men ordered all the builders to pause for a little while and rest, but they ordered the virgins not to leave the tower. And it seemed to me that the virgins were to guard the tower. After they had all paused and were resting, I spoke to the shepherd. "Why, sir," I said, "was the building of the tower not completed?"

"The tower," he said, "cannot yet be completed until its master comes and tests this building, so that if any stones are found to be defective he may replace them, for the tower is being built according to his will." . . .

And behold, a little later I saw an array of many men coming, and in the midst a man of such lofty stature that he stood taller than the tower. And the six men who had supervised the building were walking with him on his right and on his left, and with him were all those who worked on the building, and many other glorious beings were around him. And the virgins who watched the tower ran up and kissed him, and began to walk around the tower beside him. And that man inspected the building so carefully that he felt every single stone. And he held a rod in his hand, and struck every stone that had been put into the building. And when he struck the stones, some of them became black as soot, and some rough, and some cracked, and some too short, and some neither white nor black, and some became uneven and did not fit in with the other stones, and some badly spotted; these were the various kinds of defective stones found in the building. So he ordered all these to be removed from the tower and placed by the side of the tower, and other stones brought and put in their place. And the builders asked him from what mountain he wanted stones to be brought and put in their place. But he did not order them to be brought from the mountains; instead he ordered them to be brought from a certain plain that was nearby. And the plain was excavated, and brilliant square stones were found there, but some were round. And all the stones that were found in that plain were brought in and were carried through the door by the virgins. And the square stones were trimmed and set in the place of those that had been removed, but the round ones were not placed in the building, because they were too hard to shape and it took too long. So they were placed beside the tower, as though they were going to be shaped and put into the building, for they were extraordinarily brilliant.

So, when the glorious man who was lord of the whole tower had finished these things, he called the shepherd to him and handed over to him all the stones that had been removed from the building and were lying beside the tower, and said to him, "Clean these stones carefully, and use those that can fit with the others in the construction of the tower, but throw those that do not fit far away from the tower." After giving these orders to the shepherd, he left the tower, together with all those with whom he had come. And the virgins stood around the tower watching it. I said to the shepherd, "How can these stones go back into the structure of the tower after they have been rejected?"

He answered me and said, "I myself will trim the majority of these stones and put them into the building, and they will fit with the rest of the stones."

"How, sir," I said, "can they still fill the same space after they have been trimmed?"

He answered and said to me, "Those that are found to be small will be placed in the middle of the building, but those that are larger will be set on the outside and will support them."

Having spoken these things to me, he said to me, "Let us go, and after two days let us return and clean these stones and put them into the building, for everything around the tower must be cleaned up, lest the master should come unexpectedly and find things around the tower dirty and become incensed, in which case these stones will not go into the construction of the tower, and I will appear to be careless in my master's sight." And after two days we came to the tower, and he said to me, "Let us inspect all the stones, and see which ones can go into the building." . . .

Finally he came to inspect the round white stones, and he said to me, "What should we do with these stones?"

"How would I know, sir?" I said.

"Then you do not notice anything about them?"

"Sir," I said, "I do not possess this skill, nor am I a stone-cutter, nor can I understand."

"Do you not see," he said, "that they are very round, and that if I want to make them square, a great deal must be cut off of them? Yet some of them must of necessity be placed in the building."

"So if it is necessary, sir," I said, "why do you torment yourself? Why not just choose the ones you want for the building, and fit them into it?"

He chose the larger and brighter of them, and trimmed them; and the virgins took them and fitted them into the exterior portion of the building. But the rest that were left were taken and put back in the plain from which they had been brought; they were not, however, thrown away "because," he said, "there still remains a little of the tower to be built. And the master of the tower is most anxious to have these stones fitted into the building, because they are very bright." . . . And when the shepherd saw that the tower's structure was beautiful, he was extremely happy; for the tower was so well built that I admired its construction when I saw it, for it was built as if it were from a single stone, without one joint in it. And the stone looked as if it had been hewn out of the rock, for it seemed to me to be all one stone. . . .

The Shepherd Explains the Parable of the Tower

"First of all, sir," I said, "explain this to me: Who is the rock and the door?"

"This rock," he said, "and the door are the Son of God."

"How is it, sir," I said, "that the rock is old, but the door is new?" . . .

"The Son of God is far older than all his creation, with the result that he was the Father's counselor in his creation. This is why the rock is old. . . . He was revealed in the last days of the consummation; that is why the door is new, in order that those who are going to be saved may enter the kingdom of God through it. Did you notice," he said, "that the stones that came through the door have gone into the construction of the tower, but those that did not come through it were returned to their own place?"

"I noticed, sir," I said.

"In the same way," he said, "no one will enter the kingdom of God unless he receives the name of his Son. For if you want to enter some city, and that city is walled all around and has only one gate, can you enter that city except by the gate it has?"

"How, sir," I said, "could it be otherwise?"

"If, therefore, you cannot enter the city except through its gate," he said, "so too one cannot enter the kingdom of God except by the name of his Son, who was loved by him. Did you see," he said, "the multitude that was building the tower?"

"I saw them, sir," I said.

"Those," he said, "are all glorious angels. By them the Lord is walled about. But the door is the Son of God; there is only this one entrance to the Lord. No one, therefore, will go in to him in any other way than through his Son. Did you see," he said, "the six men, and the glorious and mighty man in their midst, who walked around the tower and rejected the stones from the building?"

"I saw him, sir," I said.

"The glorious man," he said, "is the Son of God, and those six are the glorious angels who surround him on his right and on his left. Not one of these glorious angels," he said, "enters God's presence without him; whoever does not receive his name will not enter the kingdom of God." . . .

"And who," I asked, "is the tower?"

"This tower," he said, "is the church."

"And who are these virgins?"

"They," he said, "are holy spirits; and there is no other way a person can be found in the kingdom of God except that they clothe him with their clothes. For if you receive only the name, but do not receive clothing from them, it does not benefit you. For these virgins are powers of the Son of God. If you bear the name but do not bear his power, you will bear his name in vain. And the stones," he said, "that you saw rejected are the ones who bore the name, but did not clothe themselves with the virgins' clothing."

"What kind of clothing do they have, sir?" I asked.

"The names themselves," he said, "are their clothing. Whoever bears the name of the Son of God ought also to bear their names, for even the Son himself bears the names of these virgins. All the stones," he said, "that you saw go into the structure of the tower, delivered by their hands and remaining in the building, are clothed with the power of these virgins. This is why you see that the tower has become a single stone with the rock. So also those who have believed in the Lord through his Son and clothe themselves with these spirits will become one spirit and one body, and their clothes will be one color. And the home of those who bear the names of the virgins is in the tower." . . .

"Hear," he said, "the names of the stronger virgins who are stationed at the corners. The first is Faith, and the second, Self-control, and the third, Power, and the fourth, Patience. And the others standing between them have these names: Sincerity, Innocence, Purity, Cheerfulness, Truth, Understanding, Harmony, and Love. The one who bears these names and the name of the Son of God will be able to enter the kingdom of God."

The Shepherd's Final Exhortations

"Mend your ways, therefore, while the tower is still being built. The Lord lives among people who love peace, for peace is truly dear to him, but he keeps his distance from the quarrelsome and those destroyed by wickedness. So return your spirit to him whole, just as you received it. . . . Do not trample on his mercy, but rather honor him, because he is so patient with your sins, and is not like you. Repent, therefore, in a way that is beneficial to you." . . .

"Carry out your ministry courageously; declare the Lord's mighty acts to every person, and you will find favor in this ministry. Whoever, therefore, walks in these command-ments will live and will have a happy life; but whoever neglects them will not live and will have an unhappy life. Tell all who are able to do right not to stop; to work at good works is beneficial to them. Moreover, I say that every person ought to be rescued from distress, for one who is in need and suffers distress in daily life is in great anguish and hardship. So whoever rescues such a person from misery wins great joy for himself. For the one who is troubled by distress of this sort is afflicted with the same anguish as one who is in chains. For many people, because of afflictions of this kind, commit suicide when they can no longer endure them. Therefore, whoever knows about the misery of someone like this and does not rescue that person commits a great sin and becomes guilty of that person's blood. Do good works, therefore, you who have received from the Lord, lest while you put off doing them the building of the tower is completed. For it is on your account that the work of building has been suspended. So unless you act quickly to do right, the tower will be completed, and you will be excluded."

Want to give this book to a friend? And keep it too? Now you can: if you pass this book on, we're happy to replace it for free. For details visit *plough.com/give.*

Plough Spiritual Guides

The Reckless Way of Love
Notes on Following Jesus
Dorothy Day

The Scandal of Redemption
When God Liberates the Poor, Saves Sinners, and Heals Nations
Oscar Romero

The Prayer God Answers
Eberhard Arnold and Richard J. Foster

Love Is Like Fire
The Confession of an Anabaptist Prisoner
Peter Riedemann

Why We Live in Community
Eberhard Arnold and Thomas Merton

Love in the Void
Where God Finds Us
Simone Weil

Plough Publishing House
845-572-3455 ◆ info@plough.com
PO BOX 398, Walden, NY 12586, USA
Robertsbridge, East Sussex TN32 5DR, UK
4188 Gwydir Highway, Elsmore, NSW 2360, Australia
www.plough.com